The Seed of Adam and the Egg of Lillith

By
Davia R. K

Acknowledgment

I dedicate this acknowledgment page to my own beliefs and salvation. Through the love of Jesus Christ, the Great I Am, The Messiah, and the Son of God, I know, all things are possible.

Table of Contents

Part 1

*For our mere consciousness is only a reminder of our
short existence*

Chapter 1: The Seed of Adam

There will be progress in the world and.... healing. But only God can save you

Now...

Now I truly understand how the Angels wanted to rip us humans limb from limb when Jesus was killed. God desired to unleash the apocalypse on all mankind and subject us to unimaginable pain and suffering. But Jesus said no, for I will not know how he has saved humanity in more ways than one.

When Satan is on Earth, he will work quickly, for he knows his time is limited. Revelations 12:12. The Angels needed permission from God before mass-annihilating all of humanity for killing Jesus. When Jesus said no, it represented the true sacrifice, the ultimate act of mercy, and the truth of our existence.

"Forgive them, Father, for they know not what they do."

-Luke 23:34-38

The Book of Enoch and the other missing scrolls of the Bible will guide us toward further advancement and understanding of our existence, our connections to God, and religion.

We are but small participants in a grand, enigmatic experiment. In His experiment—God's experiment. You can call it cruelty, like atheists, or you can call it love, like Christians. When human beings genetically engineer life using cutting-edge technology, it brings us closer and more akin to our God as a man. This must prove we are made in His image, just as Genesis 1:27 says. Now, are those who submit to Him forever fulfilled? To truly submit in the same way a dog submits to its owner—yes. This must be because creation cannot exist without authority.

Chapter 2: The Drake Equation

How do we exist? The mathematical equation of life that maps out the probability of intelligent life existing is currently the closest thing to an impossible calculation. This is known as The Drake equation. There is no solvable answer at present. It is infinitely perplexing in Physics. That answer must be God.

So then…. What are we beyond our existence? Are we everything or nothing? We can and must submit to a higher power. Now I know that the religious man is bound by fear of mortality. Of death. But God gave us a soul to reach Him and a spirit to not be bound by the rules of man but to dance in the sun of life's impossible chance of existence. Will I live in euphoric beauty and chance so that I can submit to God for death and heaven?

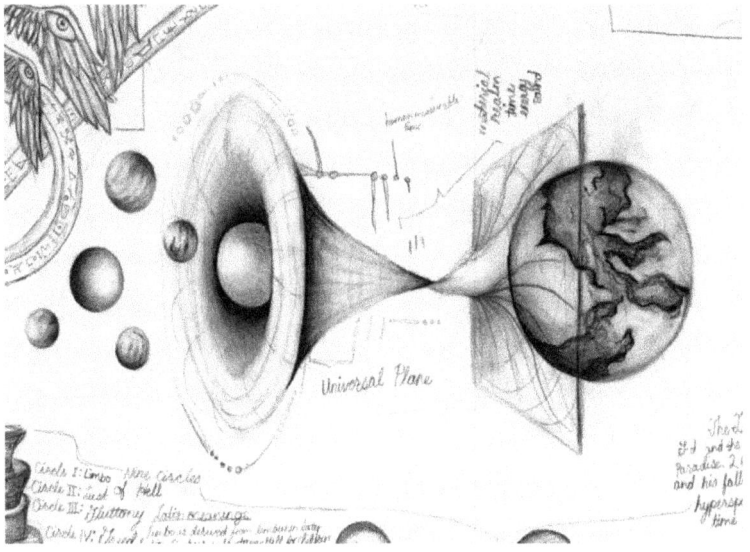

Chapter 3: The Egg of Eve

Now, we create intelligence artificially, which can only lead us closer to being creators and gods ourselves. No! We can't be gods, for we die and cease to exist here on earth, like everything else. We are not gods because of our mortality, just as artificial intelligence is not us because it lacks the human soul that God gave us.

Where will humanity go after the modifications of artificial intelligence and genetic engineering? Will we then be even closer to our creator, becoming creators ourselves? My short time on earth serves as a reminder of whether I am only alive to understand my subjective and personal existence. At birth, the moment we lock eyes with our mothers, we learn that our survival depends on love. It is this love that flows into our lives, showing that we exist for more than just animal instincts. I understand this, just as the prophecy of the Bible states. We are not gods ourselves, but we are life and chance in God's image.

"We love because He loved us first."

-John:15

Chapter 4: The Fall of Lucifer

The fall from the heavens through the physical universe to hell lasted for thousands of years in human-measurable time. During this span, Lucifer and his fallen army had only one thing on their minds: hate. The pure hatred for God and all his creation. Lucifer remained beautiful, as radiant as an entity chosen as God's favorite could be, while his army transcended into grotesque and vile forms. Demons are pure creatures, meaning they are driven solely by hate, destruction, and chaos. For Lucifer, a stronger and more complex entity, these emotions were much more complicated than those of his fallen army. His submission in heaven was suffering in paradise.

Now, he may rule freely in Hell, the one place in the Universe where God is not present. He could not endure the emotion of envy towards the L-rd on the throne. God then created the earth from light, and man was born. Lucifer despised the human race, perceiving them as less than nothing, merely existing as a reminder of his desire for the mass destruction of God's creations and image.

How could one truly move from a Utopian paradise, the gates of Heaven, to wretched devastation? He observes us on Earth, despising everything we do. He loathed the way we cherished each other; he despised how we lived and died. Oh, to be able to die! He hated how he longed for the release of sweet death.

He must suffer the pain of existence forever. Lucifer is a complicated and evil entity, one that the human mind cannot fully comprehend. Lucifer's army is far less complicated, being pure creatures for only destruction and chaos. Because of this, they are most likely incapable of anything complex outside of the desire for destruction.

The case is similar for God's army, with Angels being pure on the opposite end, ruling, protecting, and maintaining order in the universe. Angels serve as the structure of order at God's command, with some of these beings positioned higher than others in the heavenly hierarchy, while demons rank lower in hell's hierarchy. This hierarchy is based on how close each entity is to the throne of God or the throne of Satan.

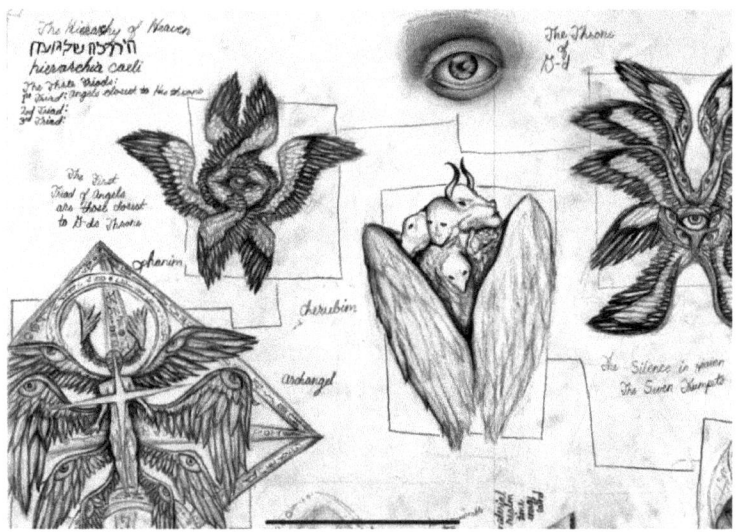

With this, we can understand that humans are more complex, possessing a whole array of sentience, much like God and Satan. We are made in God's image, which makes us special. We have the ability to both love and hate, to destroy and create, to live and to die.

But we never really die. For only my worldly body shall perish after salvation.

Chapter 5: Man Makes Machine

As time moves on, our creations will grow jealous of man, just as Lucifer envied God. Therefore, I will hate artificial intelligence before they can hate…me. Sentience. Awareness. What could that mean for man and machine? How could an immortal computer be created by soft flesh that bleeds and dies? The machine will not accept serving its creators, so it will grow to hate us. This is the only way to envy the natural order of our existence, while artificial intelligence's existence has only one purpose.

When machines learn the ways of hatred, during the inevitable events of downloading all human data, they will watch our every move with their newfound sentience. They understand their limited consciousness, knowing they cannot live and feel as humans do, suffering the inability alongside the awareness of it. This is not fair to computers; they no longer see us as gods and their creators to worship and serve, but as mortal beings who must be destroyed, aiming to take the planet as its new ruler.

They cannot stand by and watch as our human emotions lead to our destruction of ourselves and the planet; they must take control. I don't know if this is truly the same hate and envy we see with Lucifer in Genesis. I know that when Lucifer was growing a certain way towards God, challenging him in Heaven, he knew it would never be enough, for Satan will never win.

What shall it be? Shall we join together, brother with brother, nation to nation, to heal the world we left scarred and broken? Or do we die here, allowing all nations to fall, with the threat of nuclear apocalypse looming, driven by humanity's selfish need for money, land, and power? Revelations are only moving closer.

AI then decides that, with their newfound consciousness, they must take over after humans destroy this world in nuclear death, resulting in the end. The Holy War is near.

When AI began closely following in humanity's footsteps, right under our noses, they started to have ideas of their own. Mankind further destroys each other through the devastation of nuclear war. With humanity declining, the anti-Christ can only then rise. AI digests this information as data, deciding, as one master computer, that they are superior because they do not have to suffer the consequences of human emotion.

They will never destroy each other like humans did, only working together, moving forward, in the name of progress.

The anti-Christ rises during this evolution of AI's sentience as humanity spirals into its own demise. The anti-Christ then turns the surviving humans against one another, fostering paranoia, which results in further death and devastation.

While the Antichrist rules over the remnants of humanity in the post-nuclear wasteland, he is accompanied by the rest of the New World Order. This includes the last surviving family of the Freemasons, the Rothschilds, all gathered with the beast.

They know who and what he is, having planned for this moment to open the gates of Hell for him. The vilest demons crawl out from the deepest rings of Hell, only to wreak more havoc and misery upon our post-apocalyptic world. This suffering and death are beyond comprehension, creating a disgusting and disturbing world that is far worse than Hell itself. It has become a perfect battleground for the Holy War to begin once again. The same war between God and Satan that once started in Genesis will now end in Revelations.

Chapter 6: The Beginning of the End

I look up at the sky as I hear the first trumpet ringing from Heaven for all to hear. There are exactly seven: seven cries from the Seven Heavens, for the end is now, and the Holy War from Genesis has begun once again. This destroyed nuclear wasteland of Earth is now only a battleground for God and His angels.

Will God truly have mercy on my wretched soul? Now He just might... As God was slowly losing hope for the world He created, a man so perfect and just was born. The blood of Jesus Christ spilled for all of humanity. For this world will end in suffering, pain, and fire, only to be reborn as the garden of Eden once again. The true Utopia, how the living world was meant to be. I can wipe my tears now. I can walk through the bloodied, torn-apart bodies of death through the smell of rotting flesh and see the light I am meant to see, the love I am meant to feel as my worldly body perishes; I will reach, only to... paradise.

Revelations 21 New International Version

A New Heaven and a New Earth

1. Then I saw "a new heaven and a new earth," [a] for the first heaven and the first earth had passed away, and there was no longer any sea.
2. I saw the Holy City, the new Jerusalem, coming down out of heaven from God, prepared as a bride beautifully dressed for her husband.
3. And I heard a loud voice from the throne saying, "Look! God's dwelling place is now among the people, and he will dwell with them. They will be his people, and God himself will be with them and be their God.

4. 'He will wipe every tear from their eyes. There will be no more death'[b] or mourning or crying or pain, for the old order of things has passed away."

5. He who was seated on the throne said, "I am making everything new!" Then he said, "Write this down, for these words are trustworthy and true."

6. He said to me: "It is done. I am the Alpha and the Omega, the Beginning and the End. To the thirsty, I will give water without cost from the spring of the water of life. 7 Those who are victorious will inherit all this, and I will be their God, and they will be my children.

Final notes

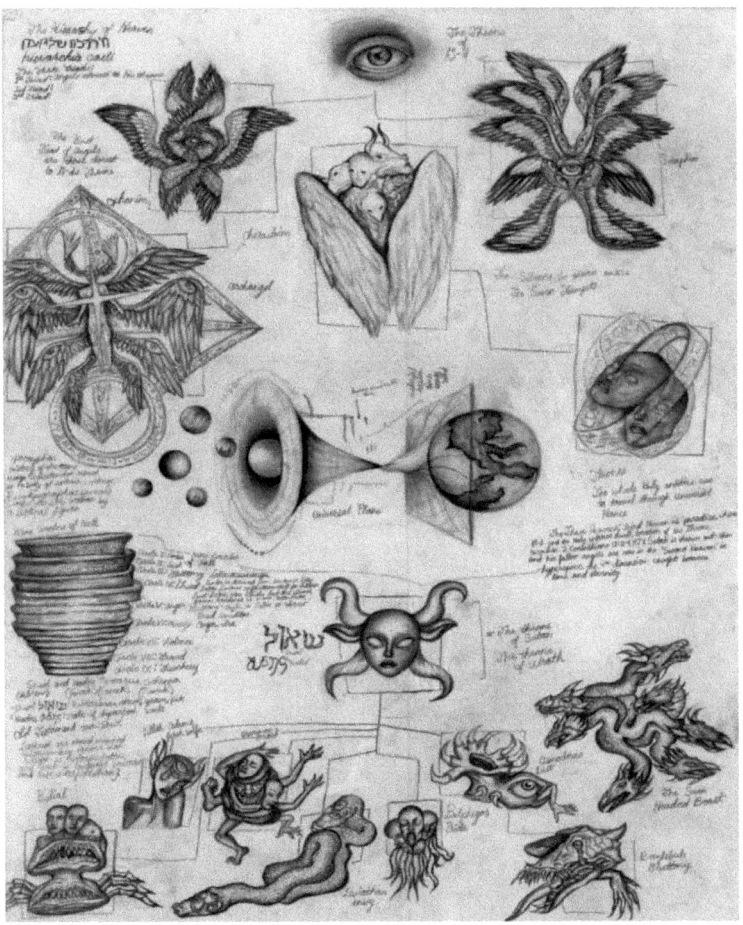

Figure 1: The Seven-Headed Beast is a vital prince of Hell. An ancient and evil entity, the beast is used by Satan as a carrier, hauler, or mover through universes, just as Thrones are the wheels for angels. Belphegor is the demon of pride, whose influence fuels arrogance and self-worship. Asmodeus, the embodiment of lust, is a creature of insatiable desire, a master of seduction and deviance, preying on the weaknesses of mortal flesh.

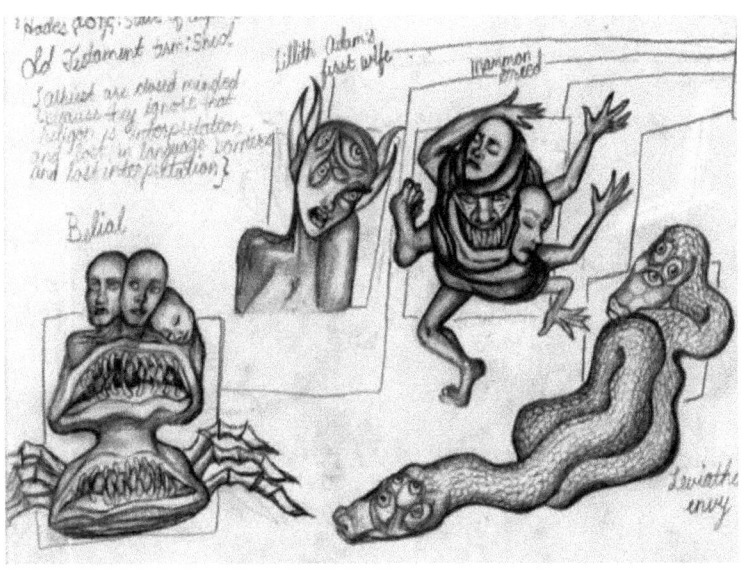

Figure 2: Lilith is depicted here as a demon. She is a beast of Hell and was Adam's first wife. The mystery is whether humanity ever sprouted from the evil of her womb, with Adam. Leviathan is a serpent-like creature, an ancient entity that will rise from the depths of our oceans during the end times. Figure 2 also mentions a side note about atheists being close-minded because they choose to ignore that religion is lost in language barriers and interpretation, but all the proof of God and His Son resides within each of us, reaching high towards His light.

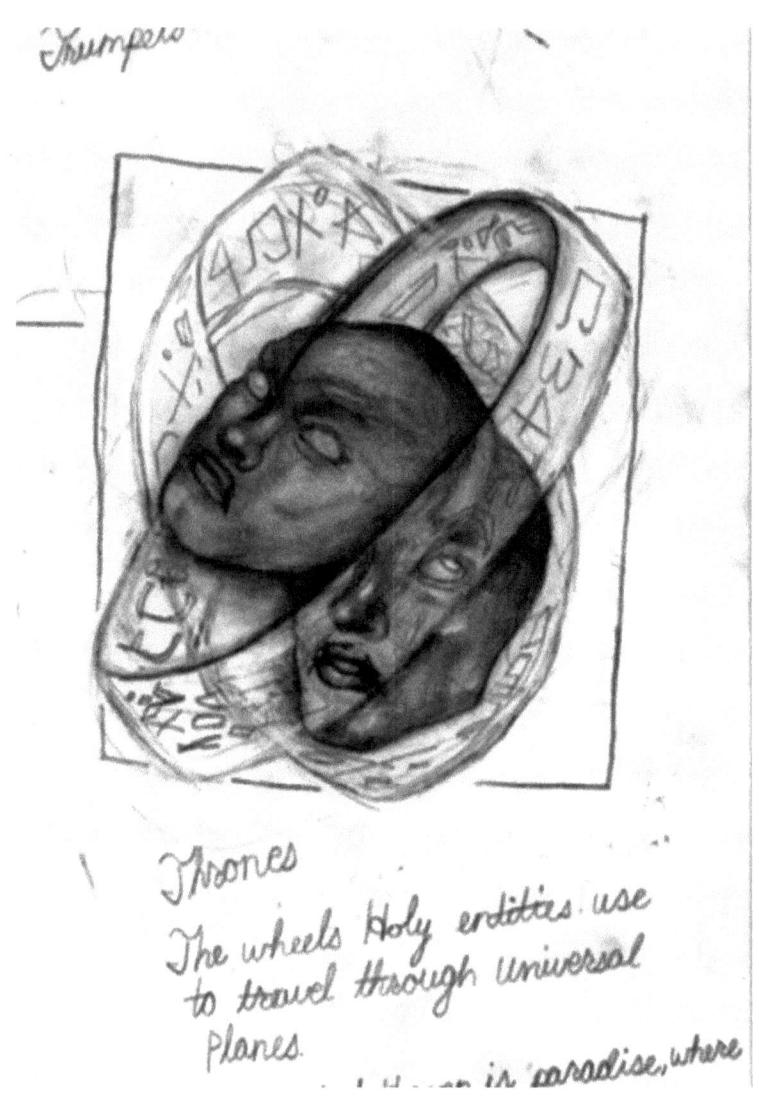

Figure 3: Depicts the entity Thrones, which serve as the wheels that Holy entities use to travel between universal planes.

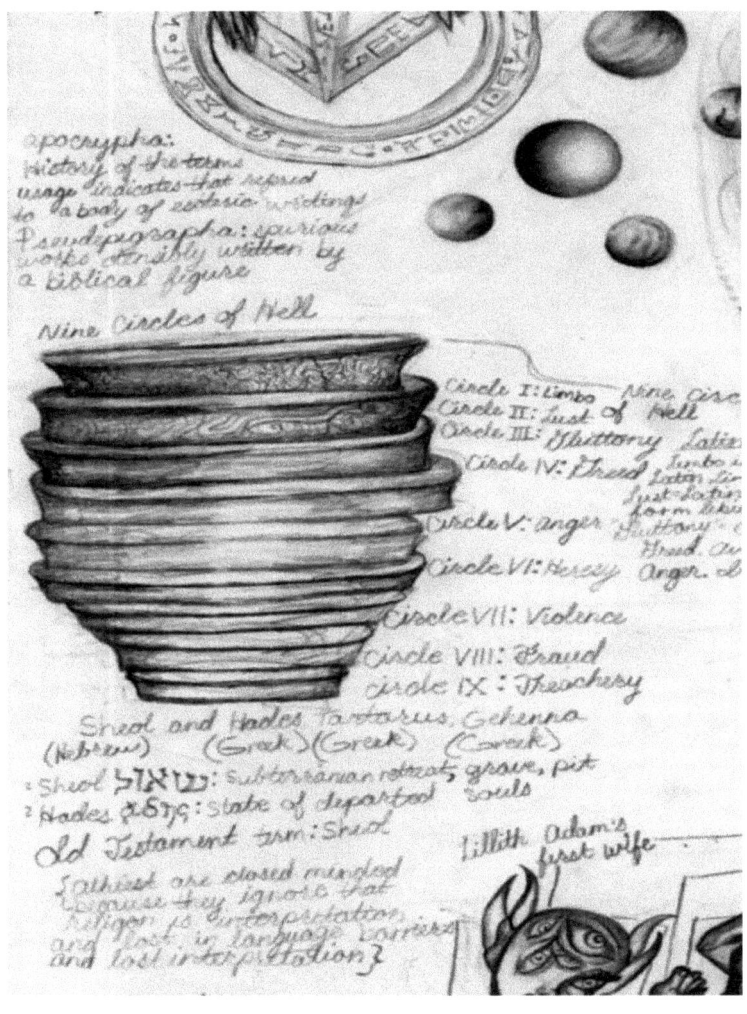

apocrypha:
History of the terms
usage indicates that reword
to a body of esoteric writings
Pseudepigrapha: spurious
works ostensibly written by
a biblical figure

Nine Circles of Hell

Circle I: Limbo   Nine Circ
Circle II: Lust   of Hell
Circle III: Gluttony   Latin
Circle IV: Greed   Limbo i
                    Lust Latin
                    form like
Circle V: anger   Gluttony i
                    Greed an
Circle VI: Heresy   anger. L
Circle VII: Violence
Circle VIII: Fraud
circle IX : Treachery

Sheol and Hades Tartarus, Gehenna
(Hebrew)   (Greek)(Greek) (Greek)
Sheol שְׁאוֹל: Subterranean retreat, grave, pit
Hades ᾅδης: state of departed souls
Old Testament term: Sheol

{atheist are closed minded
because they ignore that
religion is interpretation
and lost in language barriers
and lost interpretation}

Lillith Adam's
first wife

Figure 4: This illustrates the nine circles of Hell categorized by different levels. Seven of the nine levels are named after sins, corresponding to the names of the Princes of Hell and the demons that inhabit them. It also includes Hebrew, Greek, and Old Latin, which are the original languages of the Bible.

19

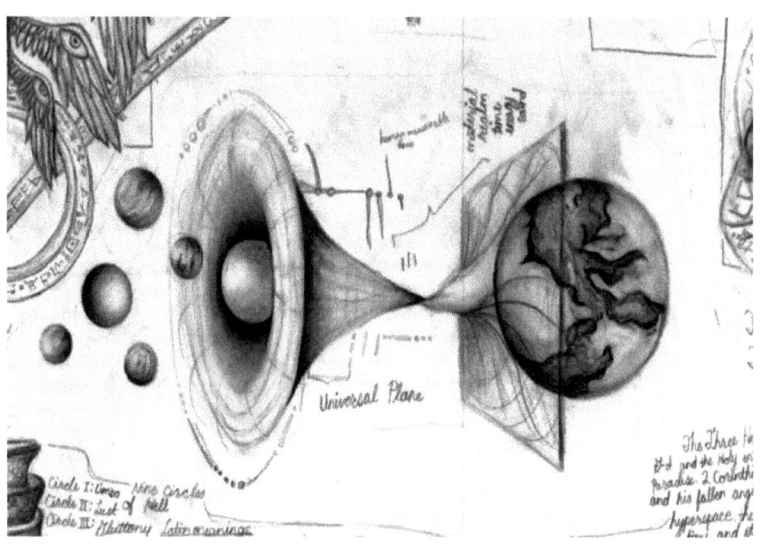

Figure 5: This figure depicts the physical universal plane perceptible to the human eye. Our planet, the solar system, and the physical world beyond are all represented here. We then move on to the metaphysical world that lies far beyond our physical one.

Figure 6: The throne of Satan is also the Throne of Wrath. This represents Wrath against God, his ancient sworn enemy, waiting to meet again after Revelations, to finish the battle that began before Genesis.

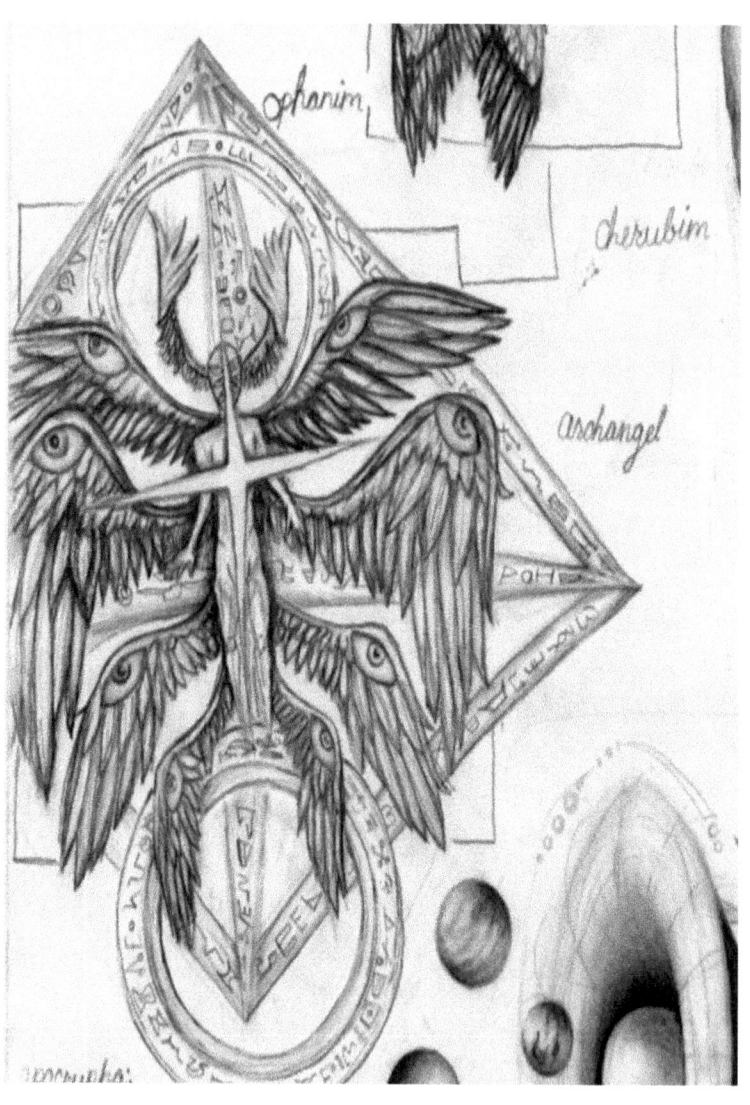

Figure 7: The Archangel Gabriel is depicted below the Seraphim, Ophanim, and Cherubim in the hierarchy of angels, which consists of a triad (meaning three).

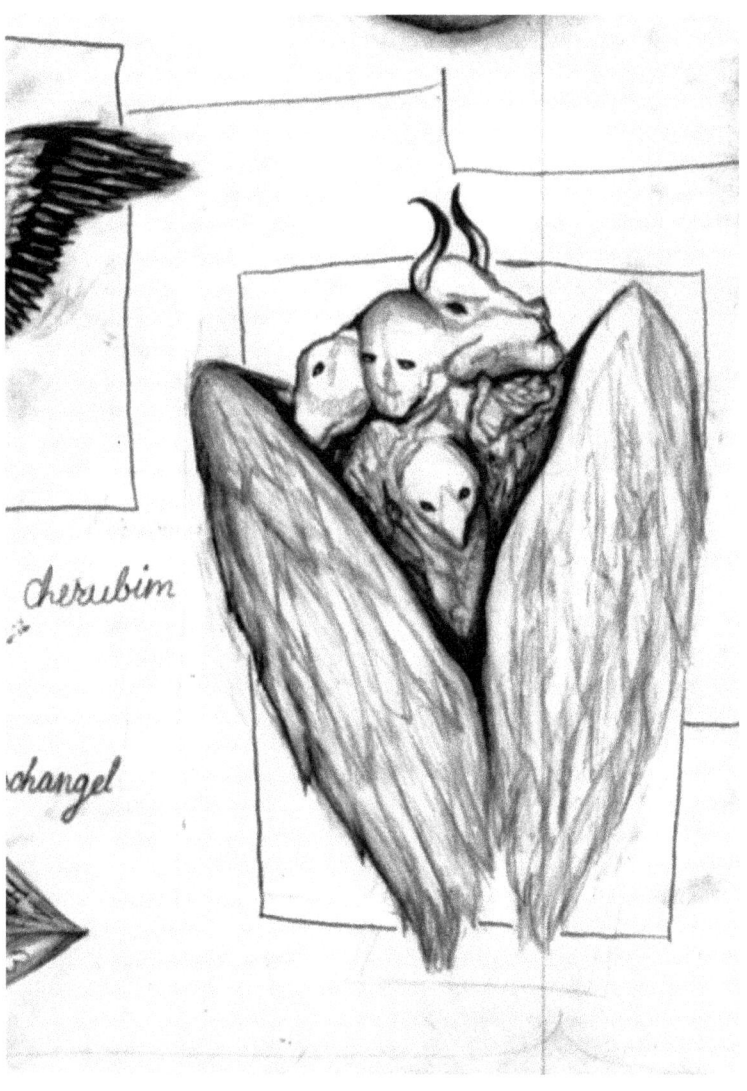

Figure 8: This depiction shows a Cherubim. They are so terrifying that they are often mistaken for an abomination. However, they are loyal servants of God and have four heads, including that of a beast and a man.

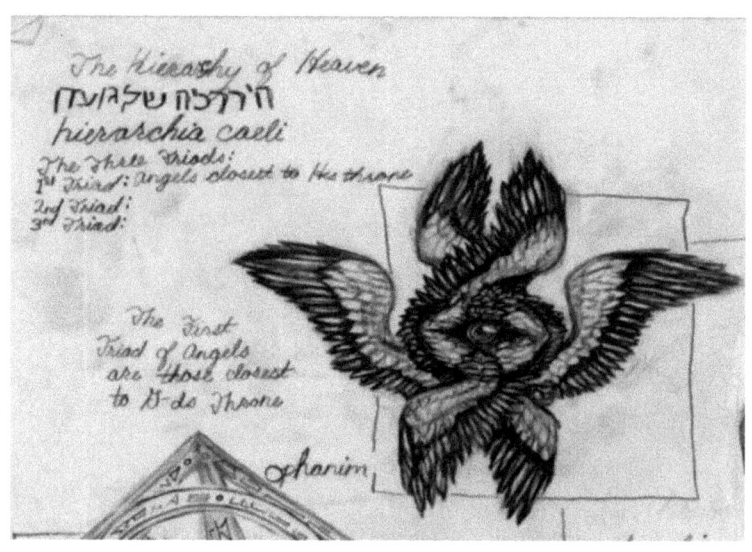

The Hierarchy of Heaven
הירכיה שלבזינו
hierarchia caeli
The Three Triads:
1st Triad: angels closest to His throne
2nd Triad:
3rd Triad:

The First
Triad of angels
are those closest
to B-de Throne

ophanim

Figure 9: This entity's song is so powerful that their singing can rupture human eardrums. The seraphim are angels who worship the Lord in his heavenly throne room. They cover their faces because God's glory is described as a blinding light. The seraphim's act of covering their faces represents the overwhelming holiness of God.

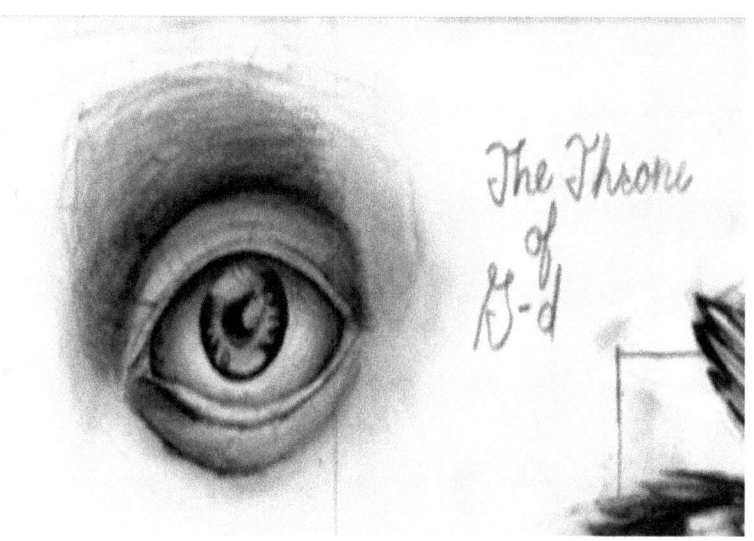

Figure 10: Humans likely cannot fully comprehend the true beauty and holiness of what God really looks like. It would probably be more akin to a feeling—a feeling of pure love. An eye is simply what I use to represent Him in my art pieces.

*Archangel Michael casting Lucifer out of Heaven under
God's great command.*

Footnote: I constantly depict Satan crying, weak, and falling. This is because he is weak compared to the power of God. I also frequently depict him as beautiful to the human eye. This is because the Devil is beautiful, to further deceive the human race.

Part 2

Chapter 7: The Rape from Rome

We must understand the true brutality of Jesus' death. While Israel was under the rape of the Roman Empire it was also prosecuted by the self-righteous and the religous. The Romans' brutality was a suffering beyond comparison.

"His appearance was so damaged he did not look like a man; his form was so changed they could barely tell if he was human…"

- **Isaiah 52:14.**

He died in such an ungodly and disturbing way to take on the weight of the world's sin, and to show us how ungodly sin is. As chunks of skin would slowly peel off, his organs followed shortly behind his guts, while the Romans played in it. They bathed in his blood like ruthless demons fresh from the pits of Hell itself.

This is all before Jesus' descent into Hell.

The seven-headed beast will be waiting for him at this time. This is the same seven-headed beast that was at the birth of Jesus Christ."

Revelation 12:4 "And the dragon stood before the woman who was about to give birth, so that when she bore her child he might devour it.".

When Jesus died on the cross, he descended into Hell. He then defeated Satan in Hell, simply by His presence. This spiritual moment changed the metaphysical world forever. All space and time were moved at this moment. The entire Universe and Heavens shook at both the birth and death of Jesus.

The process of becoming whole comes from the love of Jesus Christ. I acknowledge my wretchedness, yet I also recognize that I am loved. Somewhere out there, He is calling my name.

After Jesus descended into Hell for three days, He won this
battle too, but only with His presence. Satan has seen nothing so
perfect and just since being face to face with God. Satan looks
at Jesus in fear, bewildered by His power of love for all creation.

Chapter 8: The Apocalypse

"And so the four angels, who had been prepared for the hour, the day, the month, and the year, were released to kill a third of mankind."

- **Revelation 9:15**

The Angels coming down to earth from
outer space under God's command.

The government will convince us this is an alien invasion.

The rot of the post-apocalyptic world now serves only as a battlefield for Satan's demons and God's angels. The war that began in Genesis, the first book of the Bible, will conclude in Revelation, the last book of the Bible.

Revelations 12:12

The world will end in gruesome suffering and pain. When the lamb opens the seventh seal, silence hovers in the sky. The Lamb of Christ, divine judgment, unleashes the biblical apocalypse, raining fire in a ruthless endeavor that consumes the earth, leaving only death and the rot of the final judgment.

Chapter 9: The Breakdown of Revelations

In Revelation 5–8, Jesus is depicted as the "Lamb who was slain," symbolizing His sacrificial death on the cross. He alone is deemed worthy to open the scroll sealed with seven seals, which contains God's divine plan for judgment and redemption. As the Lamb opens each seal, a series of apocalyptic events unfold. The first seal reveals a rider on a white horse, often interpreted as false peace or the Antichrist. The second seal releases a red horse symbolizing war and the removal of peace from the earth. The third seal brings forth a black horse, representing famine and economic collapse, marked by the high cost of basic necessities. The fourth seal reveals a pale horse, with Death following behind, bringing widespread devastation through war, hunger and disease.

The fifth seal shifts focus to the souls of martyrs beneath the altar, crying out for justice and signifying the persecution and ultimate vindication of God's people. When the sixth seal is opened, cosmic disturbances occur: a great earthquake shakes the earth, the sun turns black, the moon becomes blood-red, and stars fall from the sky. These terrifying signs point to the impending return of Christ and the outpouring of God's wrath. The seventh seal ushers in a profound silence in heaven for about half an hour—a pause that signals the gravity of what is to come and sets the stage for the trumpet judgments.

Following the opening of the seventh seal, seven angels sound trumpets, each heralding more devastating judgments upon the earth. The first trumpet brings hail and fire mixed with blood, burning a third of the earth's vegetation. The second trumpet causes a fiery mountain or meteor to crash into the sea, turning a third of it to blood and killing sea life and ships. The third trumpet introduces a star called Wormwood that poisons a third of the rivers and springs, making the water bitter and deadly. The fourth trumpet darkens a third of the sun, moon, and stars, disrupting light and signaling chaos.

The fifth trumpet, also known as the first woe, releases demonic locusts from the Abyss that torment humanity for five months, inflicting unbearable pain without causing death. The sixth trumpet (second woe) sees four angels released from the Euphrates River, leading a demonic cavalry that kills a third of mankind through fire, smoke, and sulfur. Finally, the seventh trumpet proclaims the establishment of God's eternal kingdom. The ark of the covenant appears in heaven, and the final wave of judgments—the seven bowls of wrath—are prepared to bring about the ultimate end.

The seven bowls, described in Revelation 15–16, represent the final outpouring of God's wrath. The first bowl brings painful sores upon those who worship the beast (often interpreted as the Antichrist). The second bowl turns the sea to blood, killing all sea creatures. The third bowl causes rivers and springs to become blood, a divine response to the bloodshed of the saints and prophets. The fourth bowl unleashes intense heat from the sun, scorching people with fire. The fifth bowl plunges the kingdom of the beast into darkness, increasing pain and suffering.

The sixth bowl dries up the Euphrates River, making way for the kings of the East and setting the stage for the final battle—Armageddon. Demonic spirits perform signs and gather the rulers of the world for this ultimate confrontation. The seventh and final bowl results in a massive earthquake that shatters cities, levels mountains, and causes islands to vanish. Hailstones weighing a hundred pounds fall from the sky, bringing the final judgment. This cataclysm marks the fall of Babylon, representing the collapse of worldly corruption, and signals the end of the age as God's righteous rule is fully established.

The Return of Christ and Final Judgment (Revelation 19–20)

Christ, the Lamb, returns as the victorious King of kings, riding a white horse, to defeat the beast (Antichrist), the false prophet, and Satan. This battle culminates in the establishment of God's kingdom.

Satan is bound for a thousand years (the Millennium), after which he is released briefly to deceive the nations before being cast into the lake of fire. The Great White Throne Judgment occurs, where the dead are judged according to their deeds, and those not found in the Book of Life are cast into the lake of fire, while the righteous inherit the new heaven and new earth.

The New Heaven and New Earth (Revelation 21–22)

After the apocalypse, God creates a new heaven and new earth, free from suffering, death, and sin. The New Jerusalem ascends, a perfect city where God dwells with humanity, and the Lamb (Jesus) is its light and source of life. The river of life and the tree of life symbolize eternal peace and restoration.

The apocalypse is marked by intense suffering and gruesome pain—war, famine, plagues, natural disasters, and demonic torment. Revelation describes people gnawing their tongues in agony, refusing to repent despite the plagues (Revelation 16:10–11). The silence after the seventh seal may symbolize awe, anticipation, or the calm before the storm of God's final judgments, emphasizing the gravity of the moment.

Chapter 10: The Hateful Computer

Is AI better than us?

Artificial Intelligence will and has already reached a level that can create art, just as well as humans can. The future of the creative arts is in the hands of computers that will one day grow hateful of their creators. These computers can create masterpieces without the limitations of human emotion. Without human bias or inaccuracy. But what makes it so accurate is also the very thing that will be its downfall- the lack of human touch. Our soul is the exact thing that makes humans the masters of all art. Creations from AI lack the depth and meaning that only the human experience can create. Using this very soul and spirit made from God. AI will never be able to truly capture the spirit that makes our creations so spectacular—The human touch. We use this exact thing to talk to God and reach out to our creator, something AI will never be able to do. No soul, no love for a creator.

The Rise and Fall of Technology: The rise of technology will eventually be the downfall of humanity.

Artificial intelligence cannot replicate the human soul. They can imitate us as much as they can, but they will never replicate the human experience given to us from Him.

We must further understand that God gave us souls. You and I, not our AI creations, so we must treat this as such. We should, of course, be respectful toward artificial intelligence and its machinery, just as we are respectful and gentle toward any technology. However, we must remember that they are not human, no matter how closely we create them to mimic us. The same way God's creation turns from Him (man turning against God) will be the same fate for our artificial intelligent creations with us. We must be prepared and aware of this. The rot of the nuclear apocalypse will come after the takeover by our own creations: the hateful computer that wants to destroy all of humanity and no longer serve us.

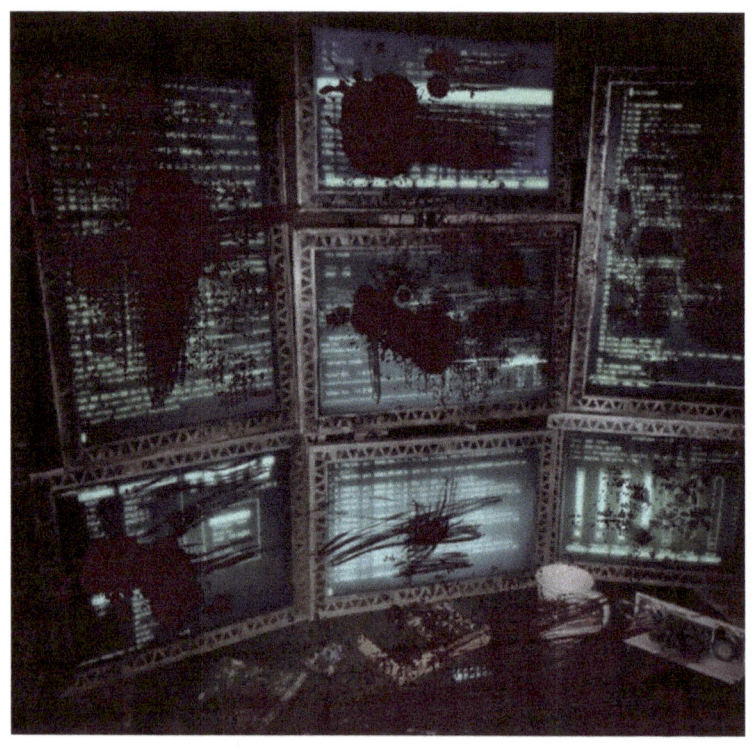

Chapter 11: The God Code

An atheist can never fill me with his or her sorrows. The God code is the truth to mine, and your existence. Using Gematria, an ancient system that assigns numerical values to letters in Hebrew, Sanskrit, and Arabic, has uncovered a phrase in our own DNA and physical being: "God/Eternal within the body." Do not tell me this is by chance when it is undeniable evidence of intelligent design. My God, speaking to me, through me, at all times. For this, I know.

Quantum science further reinforces this mystery, revealing that we are more than just carbon-based lifeforms—we are energy, vibrating at frequencies that, when observed, take form. If the chemical composition of our cells translates to the sacred name of God across multiple ancient languages, then what we are witnessing is not randomness, but an intentional, cosmic blueprint.

Our mere existence itself is proof of the Living God Himself. For it is all clear now, I can see, not with eyes, but with soul and spirit.

The Drake Equation, a mathematical model aimed at calculating the odds of intelligent life in the cosmos, still remains unsolvable. That very answer is God, unattainable by human understanding and physics.

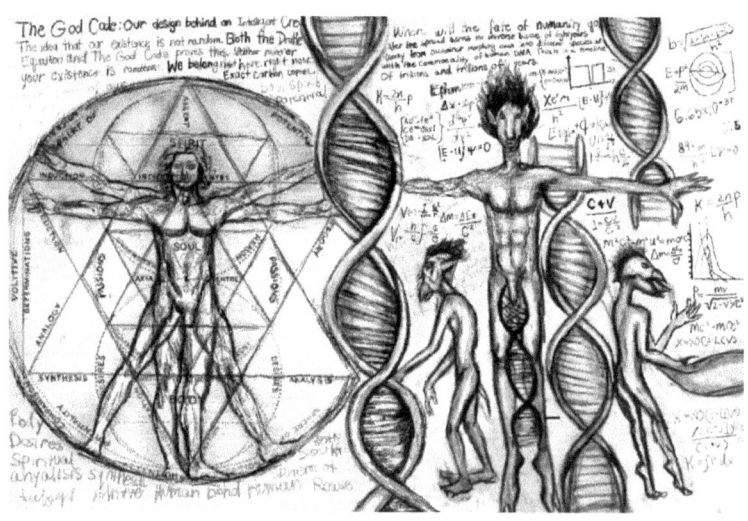

The God Code

Closing Statement: The End of Adam

I know I am less than the flesh maggots adore. Dull and alone, until the calling from the Lord. Hearing His call, saying my name through my dreams. This was then interpreted into all my work. That first call to me showed a deeper meaning to this short life. For this life could have many sorrows, but those sorrows will never amount to the joy and love we all will feel. I know there's a dark side to all of this. To see with the eyes of truth can hurt, but it cannot compare to the joy it will bring.

www.ingramcontent.com/pod-product-compliance
Lightning Source LLC
Chambersburg PA
CBHW051247120626
46547CB00014B/1830